Uniquely
Maine

D.J. Ross

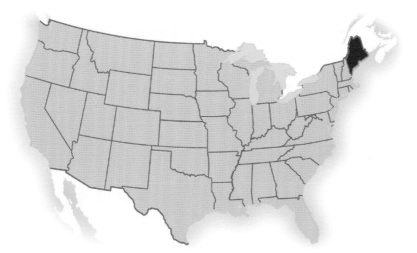

Heinemann Library
Chicago, Illinois

J
974
Ross

© 2004 Heinemann Library
a division of Reed Elsevier Inc.
Chicago, Illinois

Customer Service 888-454-2279

Visit our website at www.heinemannlibrary.com

Designed by Heinemann Library
Printed in China by WKT Company Limited

08 07 06 05 04
10 9 8 7 6 5 4 3 2 1

**Library of Congress
Cataloging-in-Publication Data**

Ross, D. J.
   Uniquely Maine / D.J. Ross.
      p. cm.—(Heinemann state studies)
   Includes index.
   ISBN 1-4034-4655-5 (lib. bdg.) — ISBN 1-4034-4724-1 (pbk.)
   1. Maine—Juvenile literature. I. Title. II. Series.
   F19.3.R67 2004
   974--dc22

                                        2004002772

Acknowledgments
Development and photo research by
BOOK BUILDERS LLC

The author and publishers are grateful to the following for permission to reproduce copyrighted material:

Cover photographs by (top, L-R): Laura C. Scheibel; George Montserrate Schwartz/Alamy; Joe Sohm/Alamy; Dorothy Keeler/Alamy **(Main):** Maine Office of Tourism; Title page (L-R): Maine Office of Tourism; Andre Jenny/Alamy; Laura C. Scheibel; Contents: Laura C. Scheibel; p. 5, 7, 8, 23, 42 Courtesy of the Maine Office of Tourism; p. 8, 41, 45 maps by IMA for BOOK BUILDERS LLC; p. 9 Folger Library/Courtesy U.S. Patent Office; p. 10, 15M, 20T, 28 Courtesy Maine State Museum; p. 11T Joe Sohm/Alamy; p. 11B Courtesy Office of the Governor; p. 12T, 12B, 14B,15T, 32, 38, 40, 41 Laura C. Scheibel; p. 13T Garth McElroy/Alamy; p. 13B Dorothy Keeler/Alamy; p. 14T Geoff du Feu/Alamy; p. 14M Pam Loudon/Alamy; p. 15B Courtesy USFWS; p. 16T TH Foto/Alamy; p. 16B Courtesy United States Mint; p. 17, 19 Maine Historical Society; p. 21 Culver Pictures; P. 22, 26, 30 James Henderson; p. 24, 27 Andre Jenny/Alamy; p. 31 Benjamin F. Fink Jr/ Alamy; p. 34 R. Capozzelli for Heinemann Library; p. 35 Courtesy University of Maine; p. 37 Sunset Avenue Productions/Alamy; p. 39 Rob Crandall/ Alamy; p. 44 Hulton/Getty.

Special thanks to James S. Henderson of the Maine State Archives for his expert comments in the preparation of this book.

Every effort has been made to contact copyright holders of any material reproduced in this book. Any omissions will be rectified in subsequent printings if notice is given to the publisher.

Cover Pictures

Top (left to right) lobsters; Stonington, Maine; Main state flag; moose **Main** Mount Katahdin and Penobscot River in Baxter State Park

Some words are shown in bold, **like this.** You can find out what they mean by looking in the glossary.

December, 2004

Contents

Uniquely Maine 4

Maine's Geography and Climate 6

Famous Firsts 9

Maine's State Symbols 11

Maine's History and People 17

The Lumber Industry 23

Maine's State Government 25

Maine's Culture 28

Maine's Food 31

Maine's Folklore and Legends 33

Maine's Sports Teams 35

Maine's Businesses and Products 37

Attractions and Landmarks 40

Map of Maine 45

Glossary 46

More Books to Read 47

Index 48

About the Author 48

Uniquely Maine

Unique means one of a kind. Located in the northeast United States, Maine is the largest of the **New England** states and ranks 39th in area among the 50 states. It is the only state that shares a border with only one other state—New Hampshire. Maine is also the easternmost state along the Atlantic coast of the United States.

ORIGIN OF THE STATE'S NAME

The name *Maine* most likely comes from early ships' logs that described the mainland from a sailor's point of view. Today, the almost 1.3 million people who live in Maine call themselves *Mainers*.

MAJOR CITIES

Portland, facing Casco Bay on the southeast coast of Maine, was settled by the English in 1633. Twelve years later, in 1645, only 45 people called Portland home. Today, it is the largest city in Maine, with a population of about 64,000.

Portland's busy waterfront is filled with sightseeing and pleasure boats, fishers and tourists, shops and restaurants.

Most of Portland is located on a narrow **peninsula.** In the 1700s Portland became a major seaport and ship-building center. Today, it is still an active port. Portland is home to the Portland Head Light, the oldest lighthouse in Maine, and one of the oldest in the United States. It was first lighted in 1791 by order of George Washington.

Augusta, first settled in 1754, is the capital of Maine. The state legislature made the decision to move to Augusta from Portland in 1827. But the legislators did not meet in the new capital until 1832. Augusta was chosen because it is near the center of the state. Augusta was chartered as a city in 1849.

To the north on the Penobscot River sits Bangor, the third-largest city in the state. Settled in 1769 by Jacob Buswell, a poor barrel maker, Bangor remained a small town until the 1820s.

Bangor is home to author Stephen King. His novels include Christine, The Shining, *and* Bag of Bones.

After statehood in 1820, Maine's northern forests fueled the expanding lumber industry. By 1830 Bangor had grown into bustling town, officially becoming a city in 1834. By the 1870s Bangor was known as the lumber capital of the world, shipping more wood products than any other city.

By 1900 however, the forests were declining, and on April 30, 1911, a great fire destroyed much of the city. After rebuilding, the city quickly became a business and cultural center.

Maine's Geography and Climate

Maine is divided into three geographic areas: the Coastal Lowlands, the Eastern New England Uplands, and the White Mountains. The Atlantic Ocean forms Maine's eastern boundary, with Canada to the north. New Hampshire borders Maine to the west.

LAND

The Coastal Lowlands begin at the Atlantic Ocean and stretch 10 to 40 miles inland. Flat, sandy beaches are common in the south, while northern beaches are often small and rocky. Thousands of years ago, this land was much higher. During the **Ice Age,** the weight of the ice pushed the land down so that only the mountaintops remained above water. These submerged mountains formed more than 400 islands off Maine's coast. The largest of these islands, named Mount Desert Island, is home to Cadillac Mountain, which rises 1,530 feet above sea level.

The Eastern New England Uplands stretch from Canada south to Connecticut. These **uplands** are about 20 to 50 miles wide. The highest areas are in the west, with **altitudes** of about 2,000 feet. In the northeastern part of the New England Uplands lies the Aroostook **Plateau.** Maine's potato crops thrive in this rich farmland. The Longfellow Mountains run through the center of this region.

The Maine White Mountain region covers northwestern Maine. This mountain range, an extension of New

Hampshire's White Mountains, is about 5 miles wide in the north and about 30 miles wide in the south.

Located at the northern end of a long hiking path called the Appalachian Trail, Maine's tallest mountain, Mount Katahdin, reaches 5,276 feet above sea level.

CLIMATE

Maine has a continental climate, meaning it has four seasons. The coastal areas have milder climates than the inland areas, but the whole state is cold in winter and warm to hot in the summer.

Winter in Maine is harsh. Temperatures dip to below 0°F. Snowfall averages 50 to 70 inches near the coast to 110 inches inland. Snow that falls near the coast usually melts in a few days, but the deep snow that falls inland sometimes lasts until May.

Because of its northern **latitude,** Maine's summer season is short. Temperatures usually reach into the 70s during the day, but sometimes soar into the 90s. Dense fog is very common along the coast in July and August because of the cool air that blows in from the Atlantic Ocean.

Average Annual Precipitation Maine

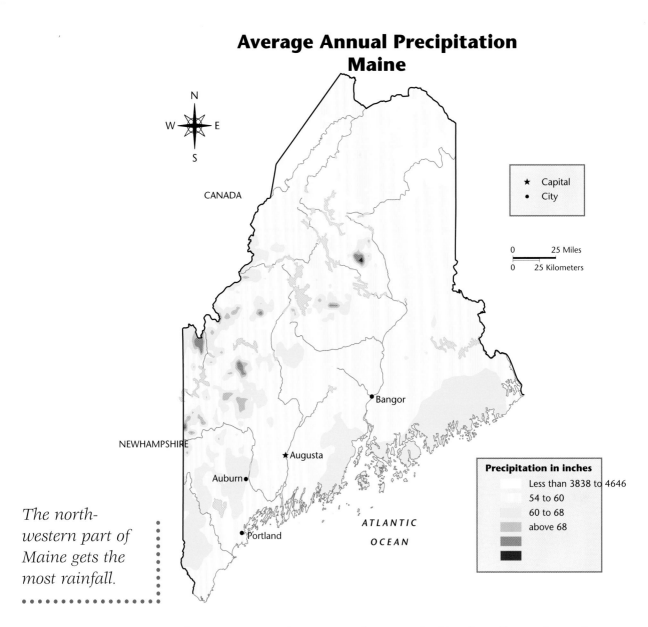

CANADA

★ Capital
• City

0   25 Miles
0   25 Kilometers

• Bangor

NEWHAMPSHIRE

★ Augusta

Auburn •

Precipitation in inches
    Less than 38   38 to 46
    54 to 60
    60 to 68
    above 68

• Portland

ATLANTIC
OCEAN

The north-western part of Maine gets the most rainfall.

Summer evenings are often cool, dipping down into the 50s. By September the temperatures reach into the 40s and by October cold Arctic air begins blowing down from Canada.

In the fall people drive to Aroostook State Park from all over the United States to watch the leaves change color.

Famous Firsts

INVENTIONS AND INNOVATIONS

In 1623 the first sawmill in the Americas was built near the town of York, Maine. Located on the Piscataqua River in southeastern Maine, the mill made ship's masts for the English navy from the area's white pine trees. The mill was the major trading area in Maine in the 1600s and early 1700s.

Born in Maine in 1838, Margaret Knight worked at a paper bag company. At that time, paper bags were envelope shaped. In 1868 she **invented** a machine that could

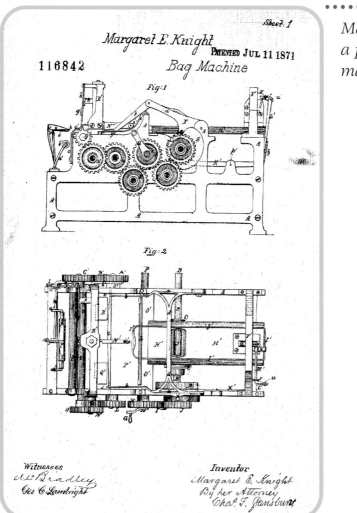

Margaret Knight received a patent for her bag-making machine in 1871.

Yankee Ingenuity

Joseph Peavey, a blacksmith from Stillwater, invented a tool that bears his name, the peavey. One day in 1857, as he watched the log drivers—the men who push and prod logs down a river or stream—try to pry the jammed logs loose, he decided to make a new, more useful tool. He went to his shop and created the peavey, which has a clasp with metal teeth, a hook, and a pick, all on the end of a long wooden handle. Log drivers soon showed how the tool quickly broke up jammed logs. The Peavey Manufacturing Company is still in Eddington, Maine.

cut, fold, and glue paper bags, like the square-bottomed bags that we still use today. Knight went on to invent dozens of other useful products. Among her **patented** inventions are a design for a window frame and a type of sewing machine.

In 1956 Maine's Kittery-Portsmouth Naval shipyard launched the USS *Swordfish,* one of the nation's first **nuclear** submarines. In 1958 the *Swordfish* became one of the first submarines to travel under the ice at the North Pole.

SOCIAL AND POLITICAL FIRSTS

Maine's new state **constitution,** written in December 1819, gave voting rights to all men—white and African American. At that time, most states prevented African Americans from voting. Maine was the first state to identify this right in its constitution.

In August 1920 the Nineteenth Amendment to the U.S. Constitution became law, granting all of the nation's women the right to vote. Because Maine held its elections in September (rather than November), Maine's women were the first to vote in the presidential election of 1920.

Maine's State Symbols

The blue background of Maine's state flag must be the same shade of blue as used in the U.S. flag.

MAINE STATE FLAG

Maine's flag shows the state's coat of arms on a blue background. This flag was adopted by the legislature in 1909, replacing an earlier design that was used between 1901 and 1909.

MAINE STATE SEAL

Maine's state seal was designed in 1820—the year of statehood. The seal's images have varied over the years but were set by law in 1919. The seal is used to emboss official state government documents.

STATE MOTTO: "DIRIGO"

Maine's motto is "Dirigo," which means "I lead" or "I direct."

STATE SONG: "STATE SONG OF MAINE"

In 1937 Roger Vinton Snow wrote the words and the music to the "State Song of Maine." It became the official state song that same year.

The images on the state seal—the shield, the moose, the pine tree, the farmer, and the sailor—are symbols of Maine's heritage.

State Song of Maine

Grand State of Maine,

proudly we sing

To tell your glories to the land,

To shout your praises till the echoes

    ring.

Should fate unkind

send us to roam,

The scent of the fragrant pines,

the tang of the salty sea

Will call us home.

Chorus

Oh, Pine Tree State,

Your woods, fields, and hills,

Your lakes, streams, and rock bound

    coast

Will ever fill our hearts with thrills,

And tho' we seek far and wide

Our search will be in vain,

To find a fairer spot on earth

Than Maine! Maine! Maine!

STATE FLOWER: WHITE PINECONE AND TASSEL

For the 1893 World's Fair in Chicago, the states were asked to choose floral emblems. Maine's legislators chose three candidates. Two, the goldenrod and apple blossom, are genuine flowers. The third choice, the pinecone and tassel, is not really a flower but **strobili.** Maine is the only state to have official state strobili. The pinecone won 10,000 of 17,000 votes. It was adopted as Maine's state flower on February 1, 1895.

The cones of the white pine are four to eight inches long and have a fragrant, gummy sap.

STATE HERB: WINTERGREEN

Wintergreen became the state herb in 1999. Growing in wooded areas, the low-growing, glossy-leafed herb blooms in July, producing white bell-shaped flowers. From fall to winter, red berries dot the plants. Native Americans crushed the leaves to use them as medicine to cure upset stomachs. To avoid paying taxes to the British, some American colonists used wintergreen in place of their regular tea during the **American Revolution** (1775–1783). Today,

Tea made from wintergreen may help soothe sore throats and upset stomachs.

wintergreen is used to flavor gum, candy, and toothpaste.

STATE BIRD: CHICKADEE

Adopted by the legislature as the state bird in 1927, the chickadee is a common sight in the Maine woods and at backyard bird feeders. The chickadee has a short neck and dark brown eyes. Its tail is long, with twelve slender feathers.

The chickadee is about five inches long.

STATE ANIMAL: MOOSE

The state legislature adopted the moose as the state animal in 1979. The largest member of the deer family, moose live in the wooded areas of Canada and the northern United States. About 30,000 moose live in Maine. Males stand more than six feet high at the shoulder and weigh between 800 and 1,400 pounds. The moose's antlers, found only on males, can reach a spread of five feet or more and are shed each year after the mating season. Females are smaller, weighing about 600 pounds, and do not grow antlers.

Moose get their food by browsing for plants in marshy areas. The best time to see a moose in the Maine forest is at dawn or dusk.

Honey can be gathered from wild bees or those kept in colonies, which may have up to 50,000 bees.

STATE INSECT: HONEYBEE

The legislature made the honeybee the state insect in 1975. Robert Towne's grade school students wrote to the state legislature to help get the honeybee adopted as Maine's state insect.

STATE CAT: MAINE COON CAT

The Maine coon cat is one of the oldest natural breeds of cat in North America. The Maine coon cat's uniqueness shows how it has adapted to a harsh climate. Its smooth, glossy coat, which is heavy and water resistant, is like that of no other cat. It is longer and thicker to protect against wet and snow. The long, bushy tail, which the cat wraps around itself when it curls up to sleep, protects it from cold winters. Big, round, tufted feet serve as "snowshoes." Maine coon cats are popular pets in Maine.

The Maine coon cat's bushy tail leads some people to think it is related to the raccoon, but it is not.

STATE BERRY: WILD BLUEBERRY

Adopted as the state berry in 1991, blueberries grow wild throughout Maine. The berries grow well in Maine's rocky soils and are not harmed by the state's severe winters. Blueberries are harvested with a special blueberry rake, which was invented more than 100 years ago by a Maine farmer, Abijah Tabbutt.

Wild blueberries grow in rocky and hilly parts of the state.

STATE TREE: WHITE PINE

The white pine was adopted as Maine's state tree by the legislature in 1945. It is the biggest conifer, or evergreen tree, in the northeastern United States and is common throughout Maine's forests. The tree's needles are soft, flexible, and bluish-green to silver-green and are arranged in bundles of five.

The white pine grows best in deep, damp, sandy, well-drained soil with plenty of sun.

STATE FISH: LANDLOCKED SALMON

The landlocked salmon is a type of Atlantic salmon. It lives in the lakes of the northern United States, but it never reaches the ocean. Landlocked salmon can weigh up to 35 pounds.

The landlocked salmon was adopted as the state fish in 1969.

STATE FOSSIL: *PERTICA QUADRIFARIA*

Pertica quadrifaria is the scientific name of a primitive plant that lived about 390 million years ago. Its **fossil** remains were discovered in 1968 in the rocks of Baxter State Park near Mount Katahdin. It was selected as the state fossil because it was first discovered in Maine. It is also rare. Well-preserved remains of the plant are found at only three other places in the world.

Quadrifaria probably reached a maximum height of about six feet, making it the largest land plant at that time.

Tourmaline was first discovered in Maine in 1820.

STATE GEMSTONE: TOURMALINE

Tourmaline became the state gemstone in 1971. Tourmaline is actually a group of several different minerals packed together. The number of different minerals determines the exact type and color of tourmaline. Schorl, a black, iron-bearing tourmaline, is the most common in Maine. Elbaite, named after the Italian island of Elba, is a less common variety of tourmaline found in Maine. Elbaite may be red, pink, green, blue, orange, or yellow. It is popular to use in jewelry.

MAINE STATE QUARTER

Minted in 2003, the Maine quarter shows Pemaquid Point Light at New Harbor along the state's rocky coast. The *Victory Chimes*, Maine's last three-masted **windjammer,** sails near the shore. The quarter is the 23rd in the series of state quarters.

A vote of the people chose the design of the Maine quarter.

Maine's History and People

The history of Maine stretches back thousands of years. Early Native American dwellers in Maine date from about 3,000 years ago. Europeans began arriving in Maine about 500 years ago.

EARLY CULTURES

The two earliest Native American groups known to live in what is today Maine are the Micmac and Abnaki (or Wabnaki). The Micmac lived in eastern Maine and are believed to have been a warlike people. The Abnaki, who lived in the western parts of the area, were farmers and fishers.

Few Native American groups remain in Maine today. The Passamaquoddy, with about 1,500 people, live on two reservations. About 1,200 Penobscot live on Indian Island in the Penobscot River at Old Town. The Micmac, with nearly 700 people, live in northern Maine.

Passamaquoddy means "people who fish for pollock," a member of the cod family.

The First Europeans

The Plymouth Company set up the first English settlement at Popham in 1607, the same year as the settlement at Jamestown, Virginia. Because the Popham colony did not survive the harsh Maine winters, Jamestown became the first permanent English settlement in America.

THE EUROPEANS

In 1614 Captain John Smith sailed along the coast of Maine and wrote a book, *Description of New England.* He encouraged people to settle in the area. In 1621 King James I granted the area to a group of **nobles.** Small settlements sprang up along the coast in the 1620s and 1630s. The area became part of the Massachusetts Colony in 1630. Although Maine attracted few European settlers, England and France fought over the ownership of Maine throughout the 1700s. Native Americans, supportive of the French, raided the English settlements, hoping to drive the settlers away.

THE AMERICAN REVOLUTION

The **American Revolution** (1775–1783) was a war between Great Britain and the American colonists. In the 1760s and 1770s, the British and the colonists disagreed over how the thirteen colonies should be governed. They also argued over taxes.

Maine's people opposed the harsh tax policies of the British government. A group of citizens led an unplanned attack on a British ship, the *Margaretta,* which was anchored in Machias Bay on Maine's east coast. Residents, armed with guns, swords, axes, and pitchforks, took over the ship and wounded the captain. The capture was the first naval battle of the American Revolution.

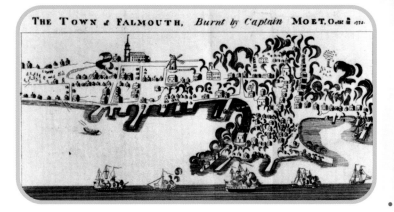

THE TOWN OF FALMOUTH, *Burnt by Captain* MOET, October 8 1775.

On October 24, 1775, the British began firing on Falmouth (now Portland) at about 9:30 in the morning and continued until nightfall.

Several small land battles flared up in Maine during the Revolutionary War. About 1,000 men lost their lives in the war and trade was almost destroyed. Maine's largest town, Falmouth (now Portland), was greatly damaged by the fighting.

STATEHOOD

Many Maine residents wanted to separate from Massachusetts and form their own state. In 1820, the U.S. Congress established Maine as the 23rd state and William King became the first governor. Under the terms of the **Missouri Compromise,** Maine joined the Union as a **free state.** The following year, Missouri entered the Union as a **slave state.** In this way, the number of free states and slave states remained equal.

Once Maine became a state, the population and the economy grew rapidly. Mining, lumbering, fishing, and shipbuilding entered a boom period. Water-powered factories sprang up along Maine's rivers. Textiles, paper, and leather products all became important manufacturing industries.

The Aroostook War

Shortly after the American Revolution ended, there was another dispute between the United States and the British. In 1839, the dispute centered on the northern boundary line of Maine. The British wanted it right through Aroostook County, and the United States was ready to fight to keep Aroostook united. Warfare never really erupted, but almost 50,000 troops were ready if it did. Maine ultimately got its border.

Colonel Joshua Chamberlain lacked any military background, but his educational experience got him to the rank of lieutenant colonel for the 20th Maine infantry regiment.

After the war, Dorothea Dix returned to helping the mentally ill.

MAINE IN THE CIVIL WAR

Massachusetts, which then included Maine, outlawed slavery in 1783. Many Mainers joined the new Republican Party in 1854, which opposed the spread of slavery. During the **Civil War** (1861–1865), about 72,000 Mainers volunteered to serve in the Union army.

The Battle of Gettysburg, in Pennsylvania, was an important turning point in the Civil War. During the second day of fighting, the 20th Maine regiment was positioned on Little Round Top, a hill overlooking the battlefield. Confederate regiments attacked, and the 20th Maine regiment fought until they were outnumbered and low on ammunition. Maine's Colonel Joshua Chamberlain ordered his men to charge the Confederates. Surprised, the Confederate troops retreated and the 20th Maine regiment held its position. This key victory helped the Union win the Battle of Gettysburg.

FAMOUS PEOPLE

Dorothea Dix (1802–1887), civil rights reformer. Born in Hampden, Dix worked for more than twenty years to improve prison and hospital conditions for the mentally ill. During the Civil War (1861–1865), she became the leader of female nurses for the Union army. She served without pay. More than 3,000 nurses worked under her direction and the quality of nursing care greatly improved—and fewer people died.

Henry Wadsworth Longfellow (1807–1882), poet. Born in Portland, and educated at Bowdoin College, Longfellow is one of the most famous American poets. Among his most well-known poems are "The Song of Hiawatha" and "The Courtship of Miles Standish." He was one of the first poets to use themes of the American landscape and Native American culture in his poems.

James G. Blaine (1830–1893), political leader. Blaine began his career as a journalist in Maine. After serving in the state legislature for three years, Blaine was elected to the U.S. House of Representatives where he served as speaker of the house from 1869 to 1875. Blaine served as secretary of state under presidents James A. Garfield (1880–1881) and Benjamin Harrison (1888–1892).

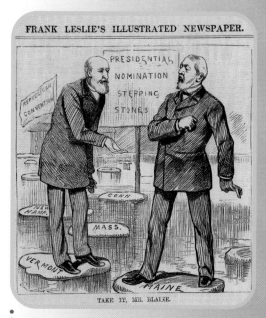

In 1884 Blaine won the Republican Party's nomination for president. In the presidential election, Grover Cleveland narrowly defeated him.

Margaret Chase Smith (1897–1995), Republican political leader. Skowhegan native Margaret Chase Smith was elected to the U.S. Senate in 1948. She became the first woman elected to this position and the first woman to serve in both the House of Representatives (1940–1948) and the Senate (1948–1972). Smith also made history by running for president in 1964, becoming the first woman seriously considered for this office.

Edmund Muskie (1914–1996), political leader. Born in Rumford, Muskie began his political career as a member of the U.S. House of Representatives. He later served two terms as Maine's governor. In 1958 Muskie was elected to the U.S. Senate, where he served for 22 years. Muskie was the Democratic Party's nominee for vice president in the 1968 election and ran for president in 1972. He became President Carter's secretary of state in 1980.

Andrew Wyeth (1917–   ), artist. Born in Chadds Ford, Pennsylvania, Wyeth was educated by his father, illustrator N.C. Wyeth. The Wyeth family spent their summers at Port Clyde, Maine, where young Andrew painted the rocky coast and the sea. Among his most famous works are *Her Room, Afternoon,* and *Around the Corner,* all of which are at the Farnsworth Art Museum in Rockport, Maine.

A statue honoring Samantha Smith outside the State Library in Augusta reminds us that young people can influence world events.

Samantha Smith (1972–1985), child peace advocate. At age ten, Samantha Smith of Manchester wrote a letter to the leader of the Soviet Union, Yuri Andropov. She asked why the Soviet Union wanted to conquer the world. Andropov wrote a long letter back to Samantha, explaining that the Soviet Union wanted peace. Smith became a celebrity and went to meet Andropov in the Soviet Union. She also met Soviet young people and discovered that they, too, wanted peace. She soon became known as an ambassador for peace. She was killed in a plane crash at age twelve.

The Lumber Industry

Maine's original forests supplied lumber for building homes and ships. Today, the forests are important contributors to the state's economy.

MAINE'S FORESTS

In the 1600s, when the first Europeans arrived in what is today Maine, dense forests of pine, spruce, and hemlock covered the much of the land. Logging began soon after settlement. The shipbuilding industry used trees as masts on the three- and four-masted schooners, a type of sailing ship.

Harvested trees served two important purposes. The straightest logs were used as ships' masts. The other trees were used to make barrels, shingles, and boards. In addition, lumbering opened the land for farming and new villages. The first communities grew where the trees had been harvested.

Bangor became the lumber capital of the world in the late 1800s. At that time, the city's mills shipped more than 246 million feet of lumber per year. Sawmills lined the Penobscot River and Kenduskeag Stream, sending

Maine's forests are protected by the Maine Forest Service, a part of the state's department of conservation.

lumber to nearby Winterport, Searsport, and Belfast for shipbuilding.

Maine's forests are producing more lumber today than ever before. But the number of jobs in the lumber industry is going down because new, more efficient technology has replaced many workers.

Paper made in mills like this one is used both by consumers and by commercial industries.

MAKING PAPER

The first paper mill in the American colonies was established in Maine in 1739. Today, Maine is home to many of the country's leading paper manufacturers, including International Paper Company. Much of the state's economy is tied to making paper and paper products.

About one-third of the raw material used to make paper is wood chips and scraps from sawmills. Another third of the material is **recycled** paper. Generally, only about one-third of the fiber used to make paper comes from new trees. Using large logs for paper is too expensive. For this reason, only trees less than eight inches in diameter are harvested for papermaking.

CONSERVATION

Maine's paper manufacturers follow strict state and federal guidelines to protect the environment. Paper plants have become more efficient. For example, the industry uses about 70 percent less water than it did 25 years ago. In addition, nearly all the chemicals used in the paper-making process are recycled. Today, harvested forests are replanted with seedlings. In this way, Maine's forests will remain for generations to come.

Maine's State Government

Maine's government is based in Augusta, the capital. A **constitution** is a plan of government. Similar to the **federal government** in Washington, D.C., Maine's government is made up of three branches—the legislative, the executive, and the judicial branch.

The state's first constitution was written in 1819, the year before Maine became a state. The constitution that governs Maine today went into effect in 1820. It promises many freedoms for Maine's people—including freedom of religion, speech, and the press. These basic rights are based on those listed in the U.S. Constitution.

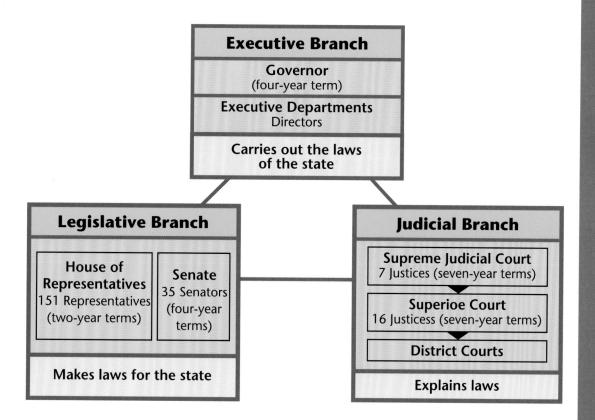

Executive Branch

Governor
(four-year term)

Executive Departments
Directors

Carries out the laws of the state

Legislative Branch

House of Representatives
151 Representatives
(two-year terms)

Senate
35 Senators
(four-year terms)

Makes laws for the state

Judicial Branch

Supreme Judicial Court
7 Justices (seven-year terms)

Superioe Court
16 Justicess (seven-year terms)

District Courts

Explains laws

THE LEGISLATIVE BRANCH

Maine's legislature makes the state's laws. It consists of two houses—the senate and the House of Representatives. The senate's 35 members are elected to four-year terms. The House's 151 members are elected to two-year terms. In addition, two nonvoting members represent the Penobscot Nation and the Passamaquoddy Tribe. State senators and representatives are limited to four two-year terms.

A bill, or proposed law, may start in either house of the legislature, except for bills about taxes. These bills must start in the House of Representatives. A bill must be approved by a **majority,** or more than half, of the members of both houses before it can be sent to the governor for approval. If the governor signs the bill, it becomes a law. If the governor **vetoes,** or rejects, the bill, it does not become a law. A two-thirds majority of the legislature may override the governor's veto.

THE EXECUTIVE BRANCH

The executive branch implements the laws and manages the state from day to day. The governor is the head

The Maine legislature first met in the State House in 1832.

Using granite from Maine quarries, workers built the capitol between 1829 and 1832. Charles Bulfinch, a famous architect who also designed the U.S. capitol in Washington, D.C., designed the original building. It was remodeled and enlarged in 1909 and 1910.

of this branch. Voters elect the governor to a four-year term of office. The governor is limited to two four-year terms.

THE JUDICIAL BRANCH

The judicial branch interprets Maine's laws. The lowest level of the state court system is the District Court. There are 31 District Courts in the state. These courts hear both civil and criminal cases and they do not use a jury. Within the District Court is the Family Division, which hears all divorce and family matters. The District Court also hears child protection cases and serves as Maine's juvenile court.

The Superior Court has jurisdiction over all criminal and civil matters that are not heard by the District Court. The Superior Court hears adult criminal cases, including murder, and civil cases, such as car accident lawsuits. The Superior Court is the only court where civil and criminal jury trials are held.

The Supreme Judicial Court is the court of final appeal. The Chief Justice serves as the head of the court. The court hears appeals of family, civil, and criminal cases from the District and Superior Courts. The court may also make decisions regarding legislative apportionment. When requested by the governor or legislature, the court also provides legal advice.

Maine's Culture

Mainers have deep cultural roots that reflect the many people who live in the state. In the northern and central parts of Maine, a French heritage is found.

FRENCH-CANADIAN TRADITIONS

In the 1600s and 1700s, France claimed part of the land that is now Maine. French trappers and traders came to the area to trade with the Native Americans. The French wanted the fur of beavers and other animals. In time, some of the French settled in the area.

In 1755 the British chased the French settlers from a part of Canada called Nova Scotia. Because Nova Scotia is barely 40 miles across the bay, many of these French settlers fled to Maine. They brought their traditions, language, and culture with them. Thus, French is often heard on the streets of Lewiston, Biddeford, and even Augusta.

Coastal as well as inland towns reflect the cultural influences of French traditions as seen in this Second Empire-style mill.

Roosevelt Campobello International Park

Franklin D. Roosevelt's family vacationed on Campobello Island off the coast of Maine—in New Brunswick, Canada. Roosevelt spent his childhood on the island, and later he brought his family there. After he became U.S. president, he spent three vacations at Campobello. In 1964 the United States and Canada created Roosevelt Campobello International Park as a unique memorial to President Roosevelt. It is one of only a few parks to be owned by two countries.

MAINE'S FESTIVALS

Maine's many festivals reflect the state's culture. One summertime favorite is the clam festival. The largest one in Maine is held in the coastal city of Yarmouth. Every July, visitors come to Yarmouth to enjoy Maine's traditional seafood—especially clams.

Another huge festival is the annual lobster festival in Rockland, usually held in August.

Mainer's use many unique words and terms.

Down East Dictionary

Mainer's term	Meaning
ayuh	yes
barrens	as in blueberry barrens where wild berries grow
blowing a gale	very windy
The County	Aroostook County in the far nort of the state
downceller	in the basement
hod	a wooden basket for carrying clams
pot	a trap, as in lobster pot
rusticator	a summer visitor
sea smoke	heavy mist rising off the water
spleeny	overly sensitive
upattic	in the attic

Visitors enjoy live entertainment, rides, attractions, and traditional crafts. Perhaps the biggest attraction, however, is the traditional New England clambake, which includes clams, lobsters, potatoes, and corn on the cob.

The Maine Potato Blossom Festival celebrates the state's long-standing potato-growing tradition. Held in Fort Fairfield in Aroostook County, the July festival features the crafts of northern Maine and great food—especially potatoes. The festival includes choosing the Potato Blossom Queen, a pageant, a parade, and fireworks and features the 'Roostook River Raft Race. It also features mashed-potato wrestling. Potatoes are celebrated again in August's Potato Feast Days in Houlton, when there are potato barrel-rolling contests and games.

MAINE'S ARTISTS AND WRITERS

Winslow Homer's home and art studio in Prout's Neck provided him with beautiful views of Maine's coast.

Maine has given the nation and the world many cultural gifts. Unique literature and art are part of Maine's cultural heritage.

Many artists came to Maine in the mid-1800s to paint and sketch. Painters, such as Fitz Hugh Lane and Thomas Cole, depicted Maine's rustic beauty. In the late 1800s and early 1900s, Winslow Homer captured Maine's rugged coastal and ocean landscapes.

Writer's, too, came to Maine for inspiration. Harriet Beecher Stowe wrote *Uncle Tom's Cabin* while she lived in Maine. Sarah Orne Jewett crafted several colorful novels and short stories in Maine, including *The Country of the Pointed Firs* and *The Foreigner*.

Maine's Food

Mainers enjoy the harvest on land and the harvest in the sea. Acres of blueberries can be eaten just as picked or prepared into a variety of dishes. Lobsters, clams, and other seafood can be eaten simply or prepared with an extravagant recipe.

BLUEBERRIES

The wild blueberry is Maine's native berry. Maine's wild blueberries grow naturally in 60,000 acres of fields that

Blueberry Cobbler

Blueberry cobbler has long been a Maine favorite. Governor Angus King (1994–2002) shared this family recipe. **Be sure to have an adult help you**.

1 pint Maine wild blueberries

1/3 cup water

1 cup white sugar, separated

1 teaspoon grated lemon rind

1 cup flour

1/4 cup brown sugar

1 teaspoon baking powder

1-1/2 tablespoon cinnamon

1/3 cup butter

Preheat oven to 350 degrees. Combine Maine wild blueberries, water, 3/4 cup white sugar, and lemon rind in a baking dish. Bring to a boil and simmer for 2 minutes. Meanwhile, combine reserved 1/4 cup white sugar with flour, brown sugar, baking powder, and cinnamon. Cut in butter until mixture is crumbly. Sprinkle crumbs over blueberry mixture. Bake approximately 25 minutes or until top is brown. Serve warm with heavy cream or vanilla ice cream.

stretch from Down East—the eastern coast—to the state's southwest corner. Adapted to Maine's rocky soils and harsh winters, wild blueberries grow well. **Commercial** farmers also raise blueberries. The berries are harvested in August.

BOUNTY FROM THE SEA

The cool waters of the Atlantic Ocean and the state's many rivers provide Maine's fishers with abundant catches. Lobsters, clams, oysters, and saltwater fish are found in the ocean. Bass, landlocked salmon, trout, pike, and perch are caught in the rivers.

Today, lobsters are caught in special lobster traps and shipped live around the world.

Maine is the leading lobster-producing state in the country. Its yearly catch is more than 22 millions pounds. Today, lobster is considered a delicacy. When Europeans first arrived in the 1600s, however, lobsters were so common that they were considered poor people's food. Lobsters were fed to servants and prisoners. Sometimes entire lobsters were buried in the soil to fertilize farm fields.

POTATOES

Potatoes are the leading **agricultural** crop in Maine. About 64,000 acres of Maine's land is devoted to growing potatoes, a crop worth more than $100 million each year. Aroos-took County, the largest county in Maine, grows about 90 percent of the state's potatoes.

Maine's Folklore and Legends

Legends and folklore are stories that are not totally true but are often based on bits of truth. These stories help people understand things that are not easily explained. They also teach lessons to younger generations. Many people pass down stories as part of their culture.

THE OLD MAN AND THE BEAR

One day an elderly Maine man was fishing on his favorite lake but not catching anything. He gave up and walked back along the shore to his fishing shack. When he got close to the front door, he saw that it was open. Being suspicious, he walked to the door and looked inside. There was a big black bear, just pulling the cork out of a molasses jug with its teeth. The molasses spilled all over the floor and the bear rubbed his paw in it, smearing it all over.

Angry, the man went to the back of the shack, put his head in the window and gave a loud yell. The bear jumped and ran out the door. The elderly man saw that the bear was holding up its front paw, still covered with molasses, so it would stay clean.

The bear ran to the lakeshore, and standing on its hind legs, it held up the paw full of molasses. Soon flies, bugs, and mosquitoes swarmed all over the sticky paw. Then the bear waded into the water with his sticky paw full of bugs. The bear held the paw out over the water. Suddenly, a big trout jumped out of the water to get to the flies. The bear gave it a swat and it landed on the shore. Then another fish jumped into the air after the flies, followed swiftly by another. Every time a fish jumped after his paw, the bear cuffed it ashore. Soon it had a large pile.

Once the bear decided he had enough fish, he waded back to shore. The man watched the bear eat a half dozen trout. But since he caught nothing, he ate only some bread and what was left of the molasses. Finally, the bear stopped eating and looked at the bushes where the man was hiding. The bear then laid the remaining fish in a row. It walked away, but it kept looking back at the bushes.

Slowly, the man crept out of the bushes and down to the shore. The bear had left six large trout for him. He looked over at the bear, who was standing at the edge of the woods. "Thanks a lot," the man called to the bear. The bear waved the now-clean paw at the old man and disappeared into the thicket. "Well," said the man, "That's the first time a bear has ever paid me for my molasses." And the man never hunted bears again.

MAINE COON CATS

Where did Maine coon cats come from? No one knows for sure. According to one legend, the coon cat was the result of a mating between a house cat and a raccoon. It does have a bushy tail and raccoonlike coloring. It can pick up food with its paws and it likes water. But it is impossible for any cat to produce young with a raccoon.

Some Mainers believe the coon cat is a cross between domestic cats brought to the United States by colonists and Angora cats introduced by New England sailors. Others think that the colonists' cats mated with Norwegian forest cats brought to the United States by the **Vikings.** We may never know for sure.

Maine's Sports Teams

Maine does not have any major-league professional sports teams. Mainers cheer for college baseball, football, and soccer teams.

COLLEGE SPORTS

The University of Maine's Black Bears play a wide variety of sports—football, volleyball, hockey, baseball, basketball, swimming, and track and field. The Black Bear teams are the most popular and widely known college teams in the state. The Black Bears play in the American East Conference. The University of Maine holds the 1993 and 1999 National Collegiate Athletic Association team national championship titles in men's ice hockey.

The Black Bears have made the NCAA Tournament field thirteen times since 1987.

Bananas, the Black Bear

The black bear has been the mascot of the University of Maine since 1914. Jeff, a black bear cub who was found on the slopes of Mount Katahdin, was loaned to the university by the local sheriff, who rescued the cub, in the hopes that it might bring good luck to the losing football team. When Jeff entered the auditorium, the surprised crowd applauded enthusiastically. Jeff gratefully stood on his head, and the crowd went "bananas." Maine went on to whip Colby College 31–6, and Maine has been "going bananas" for black bears ever since. The next year, the former track and cross-country captain Lloyd E. Houghton presented the university with its own black bear cub. Remembering Jeff's keen welcome, he suggested the cub be named Bananas. At least fifteen different black bears were named Bananas until the practice of having live mascots was banned in 1966. Today, Bananas is a cheerleader in costume.

WINTER SPORTS

Maine's winter months provide great opportunities for all types of outdoor sports—ice skating, snowboarding, ice fishing, and skiing. Mainers have been skiing since the 1800s. Today, Maine ski resorts include Sugarloaf in the western part of the state and Lonesome Pine Trails in the far north.

Maine's Businesses and Products

Maine boasts a diverse economy. Agriculture is one of the leading businesses, but industry, mining, and tourism are important to the state as well.

FOOD AND FOOD PRODUCTS

Maine is a leading producer of potatoes, blueberries, and apples. It also produces maple syrup.

Potatoes are Maine's oldest crop. They were brought to the region in the 1750s by Scots-Irish settlers. It is the largest crop, too. About 64,000 acres of the state's land is devoted to potato growing, and each acre averages 264,000 pounds of potatoes per acre each year.

Maine's blueberries are unique, because they are native to the area. Maine is the leading grower of wild, or low bush, blueberries. In other states, farmers **cultivate** high bush blueberries.

Maine is known for producing large crops of apples. Apple growing in Maine has a long history. The first known apple tree came to Maine from Massachusetts in 1788.

Orchard owners believe that warm summer days and cool fall nights make Maine apples crispier and juicier than other apples.

Maple sap is tapped only in the spring, when the sap first starts to run.

Maine farmers grow many varieties of apples—red, green, and gold. Apple growers contribute about $9 million every year to Maine's **agricultural** economy.

New England's Native Americans made the first maple syrup. European colonists improved the syrup-making process by boiling the maple sap in iron kettles. Today, Maine is a leading maple syrup–producing state. Maine maple syrup is three times sweeter than cane sugar. All Maine maple syrup is Grade A quality, as required by law. There are other **regulations** that divide the syrup into color-based groups: light amber, medium amber, dark amber, and extra dark amber. Each group has a distinct flavor and use in the kitchen. For example, medium amber syrup is used on pancakes and extra dark amber is used in dishes such as baked beans.

INDUSTRY AND MINING

Mining is another important part of Maine's economy. Maine's mines produce gems, such as tourmaline, and **industrial** material, such as sand, gravel, and stone. Maine's mining industry is valued at more than $100 million a year.

Peat

Peat is a **compound** of rotting plants and water. More than 90 percent of the world's peat is found in the **Northern Hemisphere.** And Maine holds one of the largest amounts of peat in the United States. Peat is harvested for fuel and to fertilize farm soil. Maine peat production is valued at more than $1 million each year.

TOURISM

Tourism, the second-largest industry in the state, brings about $9 billion to Maine each year. Maine actively promotes itself as a place to have fun. "Vacationland" is the motto on the state's automobile license plates. Visitors come from other states, Canada, and foreign countries to enjoy Maine's rugged coast, inland forests, and charming small towns.

Bath Iron Works

The Bath Iron Works was founded in 1884 to build ships of iron and steel, rather than of wood. The company grew successful, building steamships for companies and yachts for the wealthy.

After the United States entered World War II in 1941, the Bath Iron Works shifted all its production to naval ships. To meet the nation's wartime needs, a new naval destroyer was launched every eighteen days. By the end of the war on 1945, a record 82 ships were built at the shipyard.

After the war, Bath Iron Works began manufacturing other metal products, but never stopped making ships. In 1995, General Dynamics purchased Bath Iron Works, but its success continues. Today, the company is the lead designer and builder of certain types of guided missile destroyers.

Attractions and Landmarks

Europeans first settled in Maine almost four centuries ago, so many areas are rich in historical sites. With so much coastline, Mainers are proud of their **nautical** heritage. Harbors in Maine today are shared by **commercial** fishing boats, pleasure crafts, and sometimes an antique sailing ship or whaleboat

L.L. Bean

Mail-order business or tourist attraction? L.L. Bean is both. Founded in 1911 by L.L. Bean, who invented the Maine Hunting Shoe or "Bean Boot," the Freeport company grew quickly and became known for its high-quality products. By 1925 Bean was sending catalogs across the country, and by 1937 the small mail-order business topped $1 million in sales. The company also became famous for its guarantee—"We guarantee all items for the useful life of the product. We do not want you to have anything from L.L. Bean that is not completely satisfactory." Today, outdoors enthusiasts, shoppers, and tourists come by the busload to the famous store in Freeport.

Beginning in 1951, the L.L. Bean store stayed open 24 hours a day, 7 days a week, 365 days a year to meet its customers' needs.

Places to see in Maine

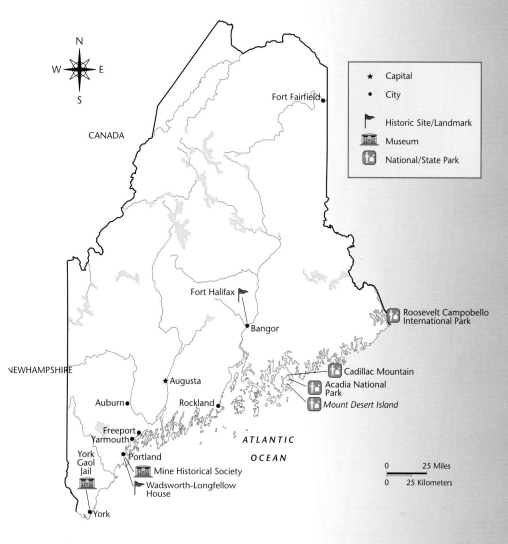

N W E S

★ Capital
• City
⚑ Historic Site/Landmark
🏛 Museum
🏛 National/State Park

Fort Fairfield •

CANADA

Fort Halifax ⚑

Roosevelt Campobello International Park

• Bangor

NEWHAMPSHIRE

★ Augusta

Cadillac Mountain

Acadia National Park

Mount Desert Island

Auburn •

Rockland •

Freeport •
Yarmouth •

ATLANTIC

OCEAN

York Gaol Jail

• Portland

Mine Historical Society

Wadsworth-Longfellow House

• York

0 ——— 25 Miles
0 ——— 25 Kilometers

OLD YORK GAOL

In 1653 an English law ordered the building of a prison for criminals and debtors. The Old York Gaol (jail) was completed in 1656. Rebuilt after a fire in 1719, it is the oldest building in the state. It also housed the gaoler (warden) and his family. The building was expanded several times. It served as the jail for all of Maine until 1760 and became a county jail when Maine became a state in 1820. Today, it is a museum. It has been restored to its 1789 appearance, and actors portray some of the jail's most famous prisoners.

The present gaol was constructed using timbers from the original gaol, which was completed in 1656.

ACADIA NATIONAL PARK

Acadia National Park is located on Mount Desert Island, off the coast of Maine. The park covers 47,633 acres of granite-domed mountains, woodlands, lakes, ponds, and ocean. Animals such as foxes, bats, porcupines, and black bears thrive in this environment. Many **species** of plants, trees, and shrubs grow on the island.

In the mid-1800s, painters and writers came to the island for inspiration and to capture the breathtaking scenery. These early visitors stayed with local farmers and fishers. By 1880, 30 hotels had sprung up on the island. Tourism was quickly becoming a major business.

In the 1880s, 1890s, and early 1900s, the families of wealthy

At 1,530 feet, Cadillac Mountain is the highest of the 26 mountains within Acadia National Park.

and powerful business leaders—such as Rockefeller, Vanderbilt, Carnegie, and Ford—came to Mount Desert Island to vacation. These wealthy men and women also helped preserve the natural splendor of the area. In 1919 Congress declared the area Lafayette National Park, and it became the first national park east of the Mississippi River. The name was changed to Acadia National Park in 1929, in remembrance of the first French settlers. Today, the park offers a wide range of activities, including camping, hiking, fishing, and biking, to the 3 million people who visit each year.

FORT HALIFAX

Fort Halifax, built in 1754, was the oldest fort in the United States before it was destroyed by a 1987 flood. It was reconstructed using many of the timbers from the original building. It stands on the fort's original site, where the Kennebec and Sebasticook rivers meet in Winslow. Fort Halifax was built at this strategic location to protect English colonial settlements along the Kennebec River. Today, it is a Maine historic site, open to visitors each summer.

Presidential Retreat

A Kennebunkport home near the water's edge—called Walker's Point—is a special place. This family home is the summer retreat for the 41st president, George H.W. Bush, and the 43rd president, George W. Bush. There is no public access to Walker's Point, however. The Secret Service makes sure that the Bush family is safe and can vacation in privacy.

THE APPALACHIAN TRAIL

The Appalachian Trail is a well-marked footpath that stretches about 2,160 miles from Mount Katahdin in Maine to Springer Mountain in Georgia. The trail follows the entire length of the Appalachian Mountains, making it one of the longest trails in the world. Hikers from around the world come to walk this long footpath from one end to the other. The trail covers the highest point in almost every state through which it passes, which makes it very challenging. Hikers can complete the trail in five to seven months.

WADSWORTH-LONGFELLOW HOUSE

Henry Wadsworth Longfellow is one of the most famous American poets. His grandfather built this house in Portland during 1785 and 1786 with bricks from Philadelphia, Pennsylvania. After the roof caught fire in 1814, Henry's father added a third story to the stately house. Longfellow lived in the house from his birth in 1807 until after he graduated from Bowdoin College in 1825. In 1901 the Maine Historical Society opened the house to visitors, making the Wadsworth-Longfellow house the first historic house museum in Maine. After a major renovation the house reopened in 2002. It was restored to look as it did in the 1850s. The remodeling cost about $700,000.

Much of Longfellow's poetry, including his famous epic poem The Song of Hiawatha, *celebrated Native American history.*

Map of Maine

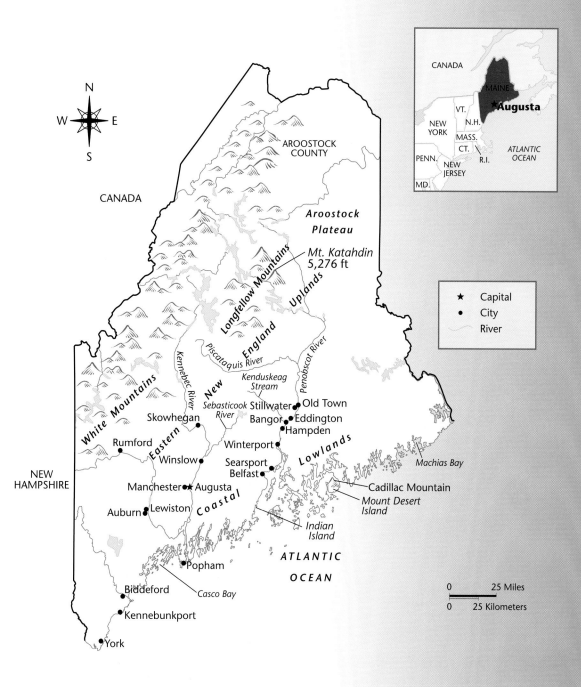

CANADA

AROOSTOCK
COUNTY

Aroostock
Plateau

Mt. Katahdin
5,276 ft

Longfellow Mountains

New England Uplands

White Mountains

Kennebec River

Piscataquis River

Kenduskeag Stream

Penobscot River

Sebasticook River

Stillwater   Old Town
Bangor   Eddington
Hampden

Skowhegan

Rumford

Winslow

Eastern

Winterport

Searsport
Belfast

Lowlands

Machias Bay

NEW
HAMPSHIRE

Manchester ★ Augusta

Cadillac Mountain
Mount Desert
Island

Auburn   Lewiston

Coastal

Indian
Island

Popham

ATLANTIC
OCEAN

Biddeford

Casco Bay

Kennebunkport

York

Inset map

CANADA

MAINE
★ Augusta

VT.
NEW
YORK   N.H.
MASS.
PENN.   CT.   R.I.
NEW
JERSEY
MD.

ATLANTIC
OCEAN

N
W   E
S

★ Capital
● City
     River

0   25 Miles
0   25 Kilometers

Glossary

agricultural the lifestyle and business of farms and farming

altitude the height of land above sea level

American Revolution the war fought from 1775 to 1783 between Great Britain and the American colonies in which the colonies won independence

Civil War the war in the United States between the Union and the Confederacy from 1861 to 1865

commercial for business only

compound mixture of two or more things that remain separate from each other

constitution written plan of government for a country or a state

cultivate to farm the land by tilling, fertilizing, watering, and other activities to grow plants or crops

federal government the national government, located in Washington, D.C.

fossil stonelike remains of an animal or plant, often found in rocks. Fossils provide information about extinct animals or plants.

free state states before and during the Civil War that did not support slavery

Ice Age severe climate changes with much longer winters and very short summers

industrial something used by business or industry

invention a machine or process that does things in a new way

latitude distance between the equator and the poles

majority a number more than one-half of the total

Missouri Compromise a law passed by Congress in 1820 that provided that Maine enter the Union as a free state

nautical related to ships and sailing

New England the original British colonies in North America

nobles people of high social rank in a country ruled by a king or a queen

Northern Hemisphere the northern half of the earth, from the equator to the North Pole

nuclear using atomic energy for power

patent government protection of inventor's ideas

peninsula a narrow strip of land surrounded by water on three sides

plateau a broad, flat, elevated area of land

recycle to use something over again instead of throwing it away

regulations government instructions about how something must be done

slave state states before and during the Civil War in which slavery was legal

species a unique kind of animal or plant

strobili part of the pine tree flower

uplands land that is lower than mountains but higher than coastal regions

veto to reject a bill passed by a legislature, thus keeping the bill from becoming law

Vikings people who lived in the area of northern Europe now known as Denmark, Norway, and Sweden

windjammer a large sailing ship having at least two masts; sometimes called a schooner

More Books to Read

Heinrichs, Anne. *Maine.* Minneapolis, Minn.: Compass Point Books, 2003.

Kent, Deborah. *Maine.* San Francisco: Children's Book Press, 2001.

Kinsey-Warnock, Natalie. *Gifts from the Sea.* New York: Alfred A. Knopf, 2003.

Knox, Barbara. *Maine.* Mankato, Minn.: Bridgestone Books, 2003.

Thompson, Kathleen. *Maine.* Austin, Tex.: Raintree/Steck-Vaughn, 1996.

Webster, Christine. *Maine.* San Francisco: Children's Book Press, 2003.

Index

Abnaki, 17
Acadia National Park, 42–43
African Americans, 10
American Revolution, 15, 18–19
Appalachian Trail, 44
apples, 37–38
Aroostook County, 30, 32
Aroostook Plateau, 6
Aroostook War, 19
artists and writers, 30, 42
Augusta, 5, 28

Bananas, 36
Bangor, 5
Bath Iron Works, 39
Baxter State Park, 15
Black Bears, 35–36
Blaine, James G., 21
blueberries, 14, 31–32, 37
Blueberry Cobbler (recipe), 31

Cadillac Mountain, 6, 42
Casco Bay, 4
Chamberlain, Col. Joshua, 20
chickadee, 13
Civil War, 20
climate, 7–8
Coastal Lowlands, 6
Cole, Thomas, 30
courts, 27
culture, 28–30

Dix, Dorothea, 20–21
Down East Dictionary, 29

Eastern New England Uplands, 6
elbaite, 16

festivals, 29–30
folklore, 33–34
food, 31–32, 37–38
Fort Halifax, 43
fossils, 15

geography, 6–7
government, 25–27
    executive branch, 26–27
    judicial branch, 27
    legislative branch, 26

Homer, Winslow, 30
honeybee, 14

industry, 38

Jewett, Sarah Orne, 30

Kennebec River, 43
Kittery-Portsmouth Naval
    Shipyard, 10
Knight, Margaret, 9

landlocked salmon, 15
Lane, Fitz Hugh, 30
L.L. Bean, 40
lobster, 32
Longfellow, Henry Wadsworth,
    21, 44
Longfellow Mountains, 6
lumber industry, 5, 9, 23–24

Maine coon cat, 14
maple syrup, 37, 38
Micmac, 17
Missouri Compromise, 19
moose, 13
Mount Desert Island, 6, 42–43
Mount Katahdin, 15, 36, 44
Muskie, Edmund, 21–22

Native Americans, 15, 17–18,
    28, 38

Old Town, 17
Old York Gaol, 41

paper bags, 9
paper manufacturing, 24
Passamaquoddy, 17
peat, 38
Peavey, Joseph, 10
Penobscot River, 5, 17, 23
Pertica quadrifaria, 15
Piscataqua River, 9
Plymouth Company, 18
Portland, 4–5, 19
Portland Head Light, 5
Potato Blossom Festival, 30
potatoes, 6, 32–33, 37

Roosevelt Campobello
    International Park, 29

slavery, 19, 20
Smith, Margaret Chase, 21
Smith, Samantha, 22
sports, 35–36
state quarter, 16
State Song of Maine (song),
    11–12
state symbols
    animal, 13
    berry, 14
    bird, 13
    cat, 14
    fish, 15
    flag, 11
    flower, 12
    fossil, 15
    gemstone, 16
    herb, 15
    insect, 14
    motto, 11
    seal, 11
    song, 11–12
    tree, 12
Stowe, Harriet Beecher, 30

tourism, 39, 42
tourmaline, 16

University of Maine, 35

voting rights, 10

Wadsworth-Longfellow House,
    44
Walker's Point, 43
White Mountains, 6, 6–7
white pine, 12
white pinecone and tassel, 12
wintergreen, 15
Wyeth, Andrew, 22

York, 9

About the Author

D.J. Ross is a writer and educator with more than 25 years of experience in education. He lived in New England and still frequently visits Maine. He now lives in the Midwest with his three basset hounds.